Songs of the Exile

David Harrison

Songs of the Exile

Acknowledgements

Some of the poems in this collection have appeared before.
sometimes in a slightly different form and/or a different title in
various publications:
'The Trout' in *Suburbs of the Mind*,
a Central Coast Poets anthology, 2004
'London Underground' and 'Study on a Motorcar Midden' in
MoodCumulus, Central Coast Poets Anthology, 2006
'Exile! (Welsh Uncle)' *Five Bells*, Spring 2006
'Deadman's Pool' and 'Truth is a Doe in the Woods' in *Leaving the Bow*,
a Central Coast Poets anthology, 2008
'A Conceit' in *Five Bells*, Summer 2010
'In Praise of Grey' in *University of the Third Age,
Sunshine Coast Magazine*, 2010
'On Holding Charlie' and 'Allure' in *Off the Path*,
a Central Coast Poets anthology, 2010
'Sydney Funnel-web' in *Australian Poets*
online poem of the week, 2010
'Poor Man Hiro', 'On the North Kent Marshes'
and 'Retreat from Turon Valley' in *Seeking the Sun*,
an anthology of the Central Coast Poets, 2012
'Allure' and 'Love Sonnet' were broadcast
on Central Coast arts, April 2012
'In Praise of Greys' won first prize in the Free Verse Category
of the writing competition of the University of the Third Age,
Sunshine Coast, 2010
Poor Man Hiro won second Prize in
the Henry Kendall Poetry Award, 2012

Songs of the Exile
ISBN 978 1 76041 348 4
Copyright © text David Harrison 2017
Cover image from the oil painting *Exclusion* by Paul Harrison

First published 2017 by
GINNINDERRA PRESS
PO Box 3461 Port Adelaide 5015 Australia
www.ginninderrapress.com.au

Contents

Introduction	9
A Conceit	13
On Viewing the Picture *Exclusion*	14
1 Exile: Temporal	**17**
An Accident of Birth	19
Childhood Eden	21
Deadman's Pool	22
Birthright	24
The Wall	25
Exile: Watershed	26
London Underground	28
Study on a Motorcar Midden	29
Mates	31
Rain From Shelter	32
Epitaph	33
Time I	34
Time II	35
Time III	36
2 Exile: Locational	**37**
Displaced	39
Australia	40
Fugitive	42
Retreat From the Turon Valley	43
The Duckmaloi	45
On Lord Howe Island	47
The Goldhawk Road	49
Aegean Dreaming	50
Exile: Land of my Fathers	51

3 Exile: Relational — 53

- embers — 55
- Passing — 56
- Mother's Rest — 57
- My Mother's Hands — 58
- Floribunda — 60
- Inosculation — 62
- Umpteenth Valentine — 63
- On Holding Charlie — 64
- Exile: Cognitive — 65

4 Exile: Natural — 67

- On the North Kent Marshes — 69
- Allure — 70
- Ocean Moods — 71
- On Lake Tekapo — 72
- Rainforest Rainbow — 74
- The Trout — 76
- I Watched An Eagle — 77
- Rainbows On My Balcony — 78
- The Dunnock's Nest — 80
- Beach Fishing at MacMasters — 81
- Tiger Snake — 83
- Sydney Funnel-web — 84
- Violet — 86
- In Praise of Grey — 87

5 Exile: Spiritual — 89

- Truth is a Doe in the Woods — 91
- The Divine Hunter — 92
- The Worm that Lives in the Eye — 93
- Accident or Design? — 95

The Love Gene	96
Forgiveness	97
Good Friday	98
Improbability	99
Unspoken	100
Poor Man Hiro	101
Grey Mutton	102
Philosopher's Stone	104
Resurrection Sunday	105
6 Exile: Whimsical	**107**
How the Frogmouth Got Its Name	109
Aliens	112
Boat People: 1800	113
Real Estate	114
The Perfect Pet	115
The Answer To All Your Storage Problems	116
Lifecycle	118
Immigrants	119
Clichés: Avoid Them Like the Plague	121
To a Girl Seen in the Park	122
Genesis by Committee	123
Zed (or Zee?)	125

Introduction

Why *Songs of the Exile*? Can I really claim to be an exile from my place of birth when I came to Australia voluntarily and could surely return to England any time I want?

The Israelites captive in Babylon were real exiles who spoke of hanging up their harps; their grief was too deep for them to sing about, but they expressed it exquisitely in the Psalms. In no way have I ever been subjected to the grief of such exile and apologise in advance to all whose grief in exile is real. However, there are ways in which we all experience the feeling of exile: a longing for a 'home' that is no longer available to us. I would go as far as to say that a majority of our most poignant poems, songs and stories reflect such a feeling of loss.

Some of the poems I have composed over the years have had this sense of exile as the conscious central theme, and 'Exile' appears in the title of some of them. However, on compiling my poems and searching for some thread that might tie together such an eclectic mix of topics, I began to see that so many of them directly or indirectly were inspired by a sense of longing for something that was missing: a sense of exclusion from where I would really like to be. This feeling was beautiful expressed by my son Paul in a series of paintings he did as an art student: painted in dark shades of ochre, brown and red, they depicted doors to a house, as seen from a cold exterior, with a warm glow emanating through glass panels. The paintings evoked a strong feeling of loneliness and exclusion, and not only for me, a proud parent. The late, great Jeffrey Smart, on a visit to an exhibition of the art students, lingered in front of Paul's pictures and remarked that they had a poetic nature. I have tried to capture my emotions about this in the poem 'On Viewing the Picture *Exclusion*'. In the case of this poem, my feeling of exile is both social and spiritual.

The latter is possibly the strongest sense of exile we experience but there are many ways in which we feel loss and exclusion: certainly in the of loss of our childhood do we not regret the loss of freshness of discovery and innocence? Are we not forced to relive that exclusion of Adam and Eve from the secure Garden? Love poems, I venture to say, are always tinged with a longing to be closer to the loved one than it is possible to be this side of paradise: an exile of the heart. Of course the loss of dear ones, parents especially, evokes such a yearning. Poems about nature, I would argue, tend to express a feeling of wanting to be elsewhere, to be closer to the perfect garden. I think this mood was very much on me when composing 'Lake Tekapo' and 'Allure'.

Am I drawing too long a bow by including whimsical poems in a collection entitled *Songs of the Exile*? Surely we laugh best at things and situations that make us think, 'There must be a better, more sensible place to be than here.' Perhaps, tolerant reader, you will see such a link in some of my lighter poems: 'Aliens' or 'The Answer to All Your Storage Problems'. In any case, dear reader, if the rest of the poems are becoming too serious, too heavy, then I hope you can find, in the last section, some light relief.

The most intense feelings of exile are undoubtedly be those in the spiritual realm. Anyone who has any sense of the spiritual at all, and I think that is everyone, must experience the feeling of longing to be part of a greater, more perfect, whole. This world, no matter how much we cling to it, must for each of us pass away. We either face this with regret or, if we believe in a God of Eternity, a feeling of finally going home. The poems of mine that speak most directly of this are probably 'Grey Mutton' and 'Resurrection Sunday'. All of us are, after all, temporary exiles in this world. Hopefully some of these poems will find a resonance with the reader's own longings.

A Conceit

words cling to my pen
like honey on a spoon
reluctant to flow
then, soft and slow,
form a golden thread
down to the bread
scrawl and scribe
a pattern of their own.
will my poem
be as sweet?

On Viewing the Picture *Exclusion*

The picture now hanging on my wall
I first saw in the gallery.
The catalogue stated, *Thirty by forty inches tall
oil on canvas.*

*A door closed, seen from outside
warm light within.*
My eyes were drawn in, I almost cried.
I had been there!

*Achieving coolness of the dark surround
with a tinge of green.*
I knew the place; had stood that very ground
and longed to enter

heard friendly chatter from within
felt so apart.
*The warm light effect is achieved by thin
layers of yellow.*

*The artist seeks to express
the agony of exclusion.*
How could he have known
my dark feelings?

That isolation was my choice.
I could at any time step in
become one with those happy voices
and lose my melancholy.

I stayed outside
though longing for the warmth
for to enter would be to conform
to His will.

Reminiscent of Holman-Hunt's pre-Raphaelite art:
'Light of the World'
Christ, with lamp, knocking at the door,
darkness within. But for me
the light was within: I without.

1

Exile: Temporal

An Accident of Birth

I have Hitler to thank
that I was born in the Forest of Dean
my mother's homeland
where she had returned for fear of the blitz
and I am thankful
for formative days
snug between England and Wales
sheltered among folk
as dependable as the oaks
as firm as the granite
who spoke a soft burr
of 'thou' and 'thissum'
and 'Ow bist ol butt'
cosseted by aunts – so many
Doll and Millie who liked their stout
Annie who disapproved
Edna and Pearl with painted nails
who danced the latest steps with me
learned so much
when not at school
of my roots in the churchyard
the plain turfed mounds
under age-gnarled yews
where slept legends:
Big Mam; Big Dad;
our Harry, brought home from Wales
on a cart
and poor little Francis

taken early of the dip*
so never play near drains
I feel still the ache in my small
legs from the walk to Speech House
where the Free-miners** held Parliament
centuries before suffrage came
to the working man
but I never did work a single day
in the dark heart of those wooded hills
so lost the rights my uncles enjoyed
who died
fighting for breath.

* diphtheria – then a common childhood killer
** Free miners – to be a free miner, a man must have been born in the Forest of Dean and work a mine for a year and a day

Childhood Eden

It was always high summer
when we went to have tea with Great Aunt Minnie,
in her garden on the common
a wonderful place
of secret glades and shady bowers
and crowded profusions of flowers
some which I knew by name:
Regal hollyhocks looked down on the masses
of blues mauves yellows,
cornflowers, pansies, marigolds,
and small pink roses in clouds
formed arches which
we ran through
along neat, narrow paths
in and out
through tall green tunnels
into bright
petal-flecked light,
and explored back again
to a quiet dank place
where a stone seat
turned green with loneliness.

We were called to sit
at the table under the great horse chestnut tree
with its white candle flowers
and the donkey begged apples over the hedge
as the warm smell of fresh scones
merged with honeysuckle.

Deadman's Pool

In the wolf-haunted forest
of my childhood
we came upon the pool
sunless, bottomless
still as the grave
black flies
hummed a nocturne
over a humped brown shape
gelled in the surface
a drowned puppy
my sister said then whispered
the terrible name
and I was held
in its empty glare –
till voices of anxious love
called us away.

Now, again on its brink,
I stare
as in a glass darkly
it gives nothing back
whatever's drawn in
remains in oblivion
and I know that if I
but say its name,
it will claim me
and number me
among the abandoned

But in this tangle-wood
where else to flee
the howling dog?

A greater love calls me:
the light shines in the darkness
the darkness has not overcome it.

Birthright

Time's touch has lain gently
on the view from Popes Hill
onto Abbots Wood
a green counterpane spread
over a crumpled bed
its oaks as old as the moon
which was bright when
we were woken from our beds
to hear the nightingale
the dark stillness of my fear
assuaged by pure notes of passion
thrills of liquid joy poured from the
trembling throat of a secret bird
hiding his loneliness in the night
you may never hear the like again
my mother said
as we walked back, searchlight beams
stabbing for bombers
among the stars.

The Wall

We came upon the wall in Abbots Wood.
So tall even my uncles could not peer over it.
Of rough grey granite
it could not be climbed
and ran through the trees
as far as we could see.
A barrier across our free forest.
My sister whispered
The nuns live in there
I have seen them through the gate
walking in the garden.
I had seen nuns too
gliding down our street
huge white hats like sails before the wind
carrying baskets.
For the poor
my mother said
but I ran and hid
because God was surely nearby.

I pulled my sister away.
Let's go gather filberts.
In case one of them should look over the wall.

I saw it again
a crumbled ruin
the garden returned to the forest.
I knew the order had long dispersed
their charity replaced
by the welfare state
but could not step over the fallen stones
for nuns had walked there.

Exile: Watershed

in Gloucestershire we sang
'rain, rain go away'
so we could play
hide and seek among the ferns
beneath the oaks
and send stick ships
to the sea
on brooks and runnels
bubbling with a child's joy

by Oxfordshire, in studied youth
we explored the bounds
of flood meadows
sweet with buttercups
there our courses met
coalesced

on the middle reaches
we paused by smooth waters
between turbulent weirs
fishermen, statue-still along the bank
hoping to finesse
silver from the muddy flow

from the Embankment
we watched together
the turbid deep
under the weight
of all that's been
carry the city's secrets
and ours
into the arms of estuary

the rivers of Babylon
were fed by exile's tears
but the river
that nurtured London and myself
was spawned in raindrops

London Underground

1945–2005

They interrupted the cricket broadcast from England
to say bombs had exploded on the Circle Line
I know it well

my father explained
how the tube train
went in a big circle round London
his city, his pride
as we waited hand in hand
for the District Line to Ealing
to visit my aunt Grace

for me, five and fresh up from the Forest
these were wonders from a story book
a squat red dragon
breathed a gust of air
and rushed from the tunnel
I leapt back from its roar
he laughed: it's only a train
the Circle Line – not ours
stairs that moved had brought us deep
under the streets

Our dad said
people came here to be safe from the bombs
in the blitz

Study on a Motorcar Midden

this then the final wayside rest
of all those weekend quests
prospecting for colour
away from the grey
workaday suburbs of our youth
whiling the miles
counting Vauxhalls, Vanguards, Fords
and Holdens like ours

landscapes sought on summer drives
now painted here
in carcass shells
of our parents discarded pride
fluent curves once polished
by father for Sunday's ride
now red encrusted
as sandstone rocks
lichen forests spread
gumnut green over iron plain
and fields of golden spores adorn
leather seats from where we saw
wind dance 'cross ripened corn
here too, the oceans drawn in
azure crazed with spangled light
on windows that once revealed
for childhood's eyes
the thrill of ocean
glimpsed between the hills

Nature's is a patient art
a decade is but a painter's stroke
all pigment is her colour chart
her canvas the broken
detritus of our brief day
on which her brush, decay
evokes vistas
of our travelled way

Mates

He walked with steady steps
and a six-pack of VB bitter
across to Arthur's place
as he did most evenings
about this time.
Exchanged a welcoming nod
sat down on the old cane chair
on the veranda
next to his mate, opened two beers
and beneath the reddening autumn sky
they complained about the land
they had helped to build
but now hardly recognised.

They reminded of times
of more gentle easy pace
when you felt cosy and at home
in this place
at peace even in times of war
safe, knowing who and where you were.
Worked hard for sure
came home weary and sore
to the wife and kids
lamb chops for dinner
apple dumplings for desert
and good clean fun on tele –
in black and white of course
and talked with mates about the better world
the young ones would enjoy.

But now you have to lock your house

Rain From Shelter

stirs
 childlike
   wonder of
     drops
    racing
   down
windowpane
  coalescing
     trails
    form an
 impression
in watery
   shades
    streamlets
    snaking
  down
  the path,
    elfin
      rivers
     where we
   watched
  childhood
    sail
      away in
      a paper
     boat
    assured
  by the
    patter on the roof.

Epitaph

How shall I be remembered?
Will a hollow remain
in the space–time continuum
a mould of me
as I once had been?

Or will the impression I leave
be as on white sand
in the bush
where is written
last night's wriggle of a snake,
the scratches of scampering claws,
a deep rut where the wallaby landed
stories told in part
gone when the next wind blows?

Or like an inscription on rock
a record for some future race
of a past corroboree
of a people supplanted?

What will I bequeath
for all that I have consumed?
Scribblings in a desert?
Will some latter-day Shelley
scoff at my arrogance
or despair at the decay?

Time I

That soulless robber of our youth
who once played the skittish friend:
amused us with foolish games while stealing away
strength, beauty, vitality
to unveil in our old age, his true face:
the slow strangler
of hope.

Time II

The arrow of entropy
whose target is chaos
and all that fleetingly appears:
order and meaning
science and art
loves and tears
mere tangles in the unfolding fabric of space
falling into incoherence.

Time III

A shuttle
thrown by the hand
of the one whose design
patterned this loom
and each life a gossamer thread
pulled through the shed*
past a moving warp
of joy, grief, hope and despair
the loathsome, the fair
until our allotted spool is spent
our fibre snapped.
Then shall we see
the whole intended fabric woven
in a myriad yarns
of varied hues and textures:
gold, cotton, flax and silk
the shining and the matt
each a vital part
of a perfected tapestry.

* shed, in weaving parlance, is the space created between the warp threads.

2

Exile: Locational

Displaced

I did not intend to leave
the land of my kindred forever
but years drifted in fresh dreams
till the strange became familiar:
blue-grey trees shed bark instead of leaves
spring in September; Easter at autumn
birds bedecked like flowers
and swans are black.

A mist of memories swirl
past woods, impossibly green
shy brown birds sing in technicolour
frostbitten mornings warmed to life
by family smiles
beside a coal fire

but even should I wish
there's no way back.

On London streets
with remembered names
lined white with buildings
which then were grimed
exotic tongues speak
cockney twang.
Under a heat-hazed sky
bare torsos bake
in parkland squares
once romantic in the city fog.
Here now the excitement
of the new I went to find
but nowhere the familiar
I left behind.

Australia

You are still that land the other side of the world
though I have dwelt within your boundaries
these thirty years
am at home here
but is that home Australia?

I've acclimatised to the summer heat – prefer it
to the damp chill of my childhood
now, see beauty in grey-green trees
currawong calls
sharp shadows
love the red baked boulders
ancient remnants of an untamed Eden
that fulfils yearnings for loneliness
while I live in cosy familiarity:
houses; gardens; streets and towns
neighbours' faces, so like
where I came from
and am spoken to in my mother tongue.
I did not emigrate but was transplanted
with all my environs to a southern clime.
In Melbourne I hear the blackbird's song.

You had already left
along with the thylacine
into the dreaming; now only glimpsed
among sandstone scrub
dimly, shimmering in outback's heat
lurking dark in crocodile pools
your heart throb
in the didgeridoo.
You are a haunted land:
the funnel-web in my shoe
tiger snake across my path
and blue-ring pulsing death
close to my naked foot remind
you are not safe Albion
but remote –
mother to a people
ancient, unknowable
that belong to you
Australia.

Fugitive

I came to this place
on a drift of desert wind
a tumbling weed
bowled along the sand
hit a stone and stayed
not from choice
but as destiny defined
here to germinate

away
from thrusting towers and ambush alleys
confounding rush through tarmac valleys
too many options, too few choices
whispered pain in thunderous voices
lonely places with many faces

found
shelter on an open plain
sustenance in a crevice
salvation on a rock
comfort from a still small voice
hope crying in the wilderness
dimensions reduced to twofold simplicity
and saw eternity
in reddened earth
a skeletal tree
where life
ended; began; dwells
will come again

Retreat From the Turon Valley

in cathedral stillness
eucalyptus incense
lies heavy
under vaulting trees
in this secret place
of the Dharug, the Gundangarra and the Wiradjuri

see
among wind-sculpted rock
and brittle scrub
the crumbling sluice wall
lichen washed
creeper strewn
snaking up the hill

listen
beyond the snap
of whip bird and
the distant whoop of wonga –
the whispered shouts
the laboured groans
of ten thousand throats
that clawed and washed
sifted exhausted soil
for grains of gold
laid there before the age
of the Dharug, the Gundangarra and Wiradjuri

sigh
and they are gone
loaded down, driven out
back to their Cathay wives
and trees of the ancients reclaim their territory
as they have done with many a convict road
miner's dam, and settler's shack
and protect
the sacred art
of the Dharug, the Gundangarra and the Wiradjuri

still
the bush crouches
waits, a hundred years or a thousand more
till we are done
then shall its roots embrace
the shells of deserted lives
and return the land
to the Dharug, the Gungangarra and the Wiradjuri

The Duckmaloi

Barry and I would drive across the range
to fish the Duckmaloi
that small river, like its name
more than passing strange
from the broad brown water beside the road
where cruised uncatchable trout
upstream and down we explored its banks
its riffles, glides and pools
where the platypus
examined us with black bead eye
declared us safe
and proceeded with its busy day
found goldfinches' nests in the tea tree tangle
while trying to retrieve our flies
watched eagles, gang gangs and kangaroos
stumbled on wombats and snakes
oh, so many snakes
the copperhead that snuggled by my boot
the tiger stretched across our path
and the enormous black, like a discarded tyre
but often just a hissing rustle through the grass
that spiced the fishing on the Duckmaloi

but we took home trout
Barry the first to resort to a worm.

Then we stopped
it was after the drought
our stream, our lively
Duckmaloi
reduced to slimy puddles
not worth the risk.

But the rains have returned
and I sat by Barry's bed
and we said that once again
when he was fit
we'd fish the Duckmaloi
and so I will and think of him
racing me to the favoured lie
through tussock and bramble
hunting trout through the heat-worn day
till the sky turns red on Bindi mount
and the owlet churrrrs over darkening pool
then he'll say, 'Wasn't that fun!'

On Lord Howe Island

If only I had been been
with those who first had seen
your cloud-capped hills
forests of feathered green
sapphire waters, rainbow reefs.

Did they feel as Adam felt –
alone with God
in a benign garden
the serpent not yet come?

Greeted by birds
that had not learnt to fear
their names, now a cenotaph
to fallen innocence:
> *Porphyrio albus*
> *Columba vitiensis godmanae*
> *Cyaneramphus novaezelandiae subflavescens*
> *Sula tasman*
> *Turdus poliocephalus vinitinctus*
> *Zosterops strenuus*
> *Aponus fuscal hullina*
> *Rhipidura fuluginosa cervina*
> *Gerygone insularis*
> *Ninox novaeseelandiae albaria*

and others that went nameless to oblivion

A paradise commemorated
on museum shelves.
Yet I glimpsed here
how heaven might be
without me to adulterate it

Will recycling our waste
and saving the wood hen
fit us to live in Eden again?

The Goldhawk Road

The tree-shade avenue of Hammersmith Grove
suddenly spills onto the scruff and chaos
that is the Goldhawk Road.
Here, by some tectonic shift
Africa has thrust into London's west.
Walk with me past the pavement café
where leather-faced men
suck thoughtfully from bronze hubble-bubbles
or sip treacle-black coffee
over an Arabic paper
by the market where they sell
falafel and dark eyes peer
from black burqas at silken underwear
along the row of shop windows ablaze
with dazzling fabrics that would look
appropriate on swaying hips
under a Congo sun
but nestled snug between
is the eel-pie-and-mash place
the last in London, opposite a raucous Irish pub
and the eatery which boasts
English food served here.

Aegean Dreaming

surely we know them
who lived millennia ago
from the things they left for us to find
a road of marble – where Paul trod
the great theatre where he was accused
of threatening trade
a library with secret passage to the brothel
communal baths and toilets even

at Knossos
the familiar women on the wall
their braided hair
prepared lovingly by their stylist
but,
beyond all, at Delphi
the magnificent young man
his horses and chariot long corroded away
yet his hand still firm but gentle on the reins
biceps tense
bulging veins
unmoved – just the flow of loose tunic
a look of relaxed concentration
sure, not arrogant
awaiting the start

these then
all that remains of ambition's of glory
images in digital cameras
only the form of the idols have changed

I photographed the Areopagus
where Paul revealed the Unknown God.

Exile: Land of my Fathers

My uncle from Abersuchen
left one afternoon
from Paddington station
with suitcase and excitement
for the Land of his Fathers
that he had last seen as a youth
though he often sang its songs
through tear-misted eyes.

Next morning he was waiting
for us at the kitchen table.
'Did you miss your connection, luv?'
my aunt enquired.
'No, I arrived all right
but it wasn't there
any more, so I came back.'

3

Exile: Relational

embers

warmth was there, round the kitchen fire
toasting crumpets in ember's glow
as we talked of our life's desire
sibling warmth by the kitchen fire

but time showed hope to be a liar
in parted ways we came to know
warmth was there, round the kitchen fire
toasting crumpets in ember's glow

Passing

she did not slip slowly away
but was suddenly gone
as if some glitch
in hardware wiped all
that had been stored
precious RAM and ROM
now somewhere –
inaccessible
until a higher expertise
will retrieve her

Mother's Rest

Finally
she has her longed-for rest
all bustle and bother gone
cares that beset her livelong day
no more steal her sleep.
the dust she chased
with cloth and hoover
is settled on shelf and floor
the eternal conundrum:
how to feed the family?
now resolved
they'll eat the funeral cake
concerns once nurtured, are homeless orphans
will David's cold turn to croup?
will Babs marry that nincompoop?
why can't Ted get a proper job?
he may end like his uncle Bob.
then it was the grandkids turn
others must adopt them now
they have no place under the stone
inscribed with our love and loss.

My Mother's Hands

I hold them
once so smooth, now misshapen twigs
these knots and burrs were joints and knuckles.
The thumbs twist grotesquely across palms
shrivelled as autumn leaves –
moist with tears, mine not hers.
Don't they hurt at all?
Once they were afire but even pain burns out.

I feel them as they were:
stroking my brow, soothing my anxiety
soft yet strong, quick and capable
sewing for me, knitting for me
baking for me, playing for me
with wonderful dexterity.
How did I not see the creeping agony?
Was it I that stole the use from them?
When I left, her hand
like a gale-blown umbrella
opened wide in a loving, longing wave
then, for the last time
I saw wetness in her eyes.

I remember myself at play with gloves
found in her dressing table drawer:
linen; satin; kidskin; velvet; long and short
all so neatly made.
I wriggle my fingers far inside and ask:
what were they for? She recites again,
These were for Sunday best
and these went with the dress
I wore when I met your dad
the white were worn on my wedding day
                now put them away.
Memories had soured, pain infused
stiffening her frame until
all love consumed, all feeling gone
only a distorted shell to survive inside.
And I never noticed until now.
How I wish she would cry with me.

Floribunda

If my love for you were a flower
it could be a rose
of deep deep red
for passion
but a rose is borne
on a stem with thorns
that is not my love for you

or my love could be
a water lily
pink or yellow
floating serene
but they flower
but a day or two –
my love's does not fade so soon

a sunflower perhaps
tall and boldly
happy in summer's warmth
but hangs its head in shame
when heat is gone
my love is more resilient

a tulip? perfect in beauty
balance and shape?
a precocious crocus
so early to bloom?
or a spring abundance
of bluebells, purpling the woodland?
or the simple sincerity
of the pansy?
the everlasting daisy?

my love is a whole bouquet.

Inosculation

To say I love you is to say I breathe
It is not now an act of choice or will
No gift for me to withhold or bequeath
But a need that to live I must fulfil
For we, like two trees planted close have grown
With roots intermingled and limbs entwined
Skin chafed together as each wind has blown
Until branches merged, cambium combined
Was it the plan of the Immortal Grower
To pleach us thus, so that our souls enlace
But give your beauty its separate flower?
The exquisite bound to the commonplace.

Then together let's grow, become love's shrine
That the Gardener graft us to His sacred vine.

Inosculation: of separate plants becoming joined by intertwining or rubbing together of limbs that become fused as they grow; a form of natural grafting.

Cambium: the vital layer of tissue in plant stems that is responsible for growth and differentiation of new wood; it is the cambium that must be joined in grafting.

Pleach: the technique, popular in older formal gardens, of forming trellises and bowers by intertwining stems of separate plants so that they inosculate.

Umpteenth Valentine

That old thief time steals softly.
Can love so long remain
and yet retain
the thrill of spring?
Or must passing years
render the familiar stale?

And yet
treasured love does not grow old
is like a chest of gold
the miser
opens each day
to pray in wonder
that all this should be his.

On Holding Charlie

son of my son
blood of my blood
what inheritance
will you have from me?
which quarter of my vital coil
is entwined in each cell
of your emerging being?
what part of your phenotype
will be moulded to my form?
hush dear babe
rest assured
your female line is strong
has made you beautiful
and yet do I see
a familiarity of the mirror?
a thought-laden look?
let it not be my melancholy
but rather the hope
some scientists claim
is borne in the genes of sapient man
and makes him praise the creator
of such a sacred thing

that, sweet child
is all of myself that I would leave to you
that you know
the love of the Son

Exile: Cognitive

faces speak of memories
greet me as if we've met before
I have learnt to accept
their need for recognition

in the convolutions of my brain
are kept those I knew, though told
they have metamorphosed
to visitors bringing flowers

I return to where I'm known
a more secure reality
relive deeds now more aptly done
with those I loved; they do not come

I only know this clouded life
is not the one where I belong
the future is already gone
all pasts and presents admix to one.

4

Exile: Natural

On the North Kent Marshes

I have heard the curlew cry
alone, alone
where the grey satin mud spreads
to meet a low grey sky and the estuary
a distant line of steel.
Out there, flocks of knot rise, flicker and wheel
settle back into a congealed silence
torn, by the curlew cry
on an icy breeze from a Viking sea
that stirs no leaf nor blade but
miasmic air too vast to fill
and carries still
the cries of hunters long ago
that chased the brant, the teal. the garganey
across that slippery plain
and many a careless tread
held by the sucking ooze
until fast, the flowing tide
slid across the surface slime
filled each shell and hollow
and the curlew cry
a requiem.

I sought the curlew cry
at the edge of emptiness
all vanities drained away
and bare truth lay
shapeless, soundless
grey

and the curlew cried
credo, credo.

Allure

it is not just the fur and feather flies
named by poets
Wickham's Fancy; Greenwell's Glory
Teal and Blue; Mallard and Claret
nor the wisp thin leader
the silk-smooth line
the elegant taper of rod
or ratchet-tune of the reel
though each is a joy
not the silver swift river
now deeply, seriously gliding
now skipping, chuckling
over round brown stones
under green bowers
or the birds, or the tranquillity
not even
the thrilling heavy throb of
of a resisting fish
which, if hunger had been the need
I would not have freed

deeper longings bring me
to stand in the
crystal stream
feel it embrace my thighs
send my weighted nymph
into its depths
flow with it through
every curl and swirl
to where the wild trout lies
      and be complete

Ocean Moods

At times she laps the shore
lackadaisical

some days she plays
in soft surging sprays
urges surfers to the land
and tries to wet the toes
of those who stroll the strand

other tides she shows her malicious side
curls, swirls, and churns
hisses, with vicious intent
would drown
any who'd brave her frown

then there's the excitement of her rage
when rampant, wave on wave on wave
dash in foaming apoplexy
thrash the hated beach
spits salt spray
at all beyond her reach
roaring ferocious threats
and deep into the darkness
of her night I, in my bed
thrill to each convulsive growl
knowing tomorrow
all passion spent
she will caress the sand

On Lake Tekapo

I have read
that it was a collision
of great tectonic plates
that buckled and folded
the earth's crust like crinkled paper
to form heights whose majesty
enthrals the coldest soul.

I understand
that over ages long
wind, rain, ice and sun
sculptured the graceful peaks
smoothed the saddles and slopes
made curves more sensual
than a Roman marble.

I have learned
how elevation causes clouds
to form and rise spill precipitation
that thinning air chills, spreads
on mountain crowns
a white coverlet
pristine as a dove's breast.

I accept
that it was the creep of ancient ice
that carved from rock and scree
this perfect hollow
nestled gently
in the arms of the hills

I know
that science explains
how the frigid water
from glacial streams
refracts; selects spectral rays
of this precise green
more lovely
than a turquoise gem
set perfect by the jeweller's art

All this I believe.
But who made it beautiful?

Rainforest Rainbow

Winter at O'Reilley's:
it is raining of course
the forest silently dripping
an odour of dank mystery.
From high, high
up amid tangled vines
staccato cries punctuate
cathedral stillness
down here nothing moves
except a shuffle in leaf litter.
The forest has time in abundance
a shoot of the strangler fig
searches down to
root by the buttress
of the great mahogany
in a century or two
it will squeeze life from its prey
like the python we saw
lazily digesting two
pademelon-sized lumps.
Only the stream hurries
launches from the lip
of the cliff to form
a silvery gash down
through the steep green
into secret understorey
from where cascades
rich round
notes of a lyre.

Across the far misted hillside
is painted in watercolour
the spectral sign
of redemption.
Are we forgiven
our trespass here?
Appropriate then the
burnished gold
on the wing of the bower.

The Trout

The great blue dragonflies
helicoptered lazily
in the doze of after lunch
above the flat still surface of the pond
which burst with a silver shower
and a vibrating golden bar
fish finned, strained up
snapped clean a dragonfly
hung there forever in my mind
then splashed back noisily in the cathedral silence
of the woods
the rocking water alone
showed that it was true.

I Watched an Eagle

chased by a murder of crows
sway on blanket wings
unbothered
a few heavy beats
as they pressed too close
outpaced these pests.
They looked so small
beside his nobility
so black against his purity
had he wished, he had but to roll
and snatch one from the air
his talons tear
at the dark heart.
But this day the King
was in a forgiving vein
effortlessly flew
to his space in the sky
and hung there
Victory
over the placid sea.

Rainbows On My Balcony

Lorikeets are true natives of Sydney
gaudy, brash and bold.
Three hang on a palm-flower frond
combing nectar with hairy tongues.
Nectar is appropriate ambrosia
for creatures that look as if they have fallen
from a jewelled paradise
purple, fire-orange and green
combinations that
were they employed by mere mortals
in paints or fabric, would nauseate
yet, on these, they look magnificent.
A pair perch close on the balcony rail
begin a complex dance. The male
I assume, for they look alike, leads:

slowly, deliberately – stretches to full height – hops to up
to his *amoureuse* – thrusts out his yellow waistcoat – she
pretends not to see – bobs his purple head under her eye –
flashes his wings then…saunters off in a sudden fit of apathy
– she follows, sits close – they nibble each other's neck with
mounting ardour then…passion spent, sit and preen.

Suddenly swoops in the mob
a vivid maelstrom
of squawking, screeching colour.
Just as nature compensated the
sombre dressed nightingale
with magical melodic song
she balanced the kaleidoscope vivacity of the lorikeet
with a voice of grating iron gates.

In my native England
birds quietly and coyly creep
trying not to be seen.
These Australian parrots can't be, won't be, missed.
Surely they defy Darwin.
How can such brilliance hide from hawks?
Now, in a swirling, whirling rainbow cloud
they fly up into a tall gum tree and
among lucent, sun-dappled leaves –
disappear.

The Dunnock's Nest

deep in the privet hedge
snug among crowding stems
lay a thing
meticulous
a spiky bowl
of dry, pliable twigs
but inside, a cosy cup
of fine hair and down
each strand perfectly spun
by the industry of a
dull brown bird
and there, incongruously
in this dun world
a smooth blue egg
as if the sky had been peeled
to form the shell

Beach Fishing at MacMasters

I stand with little expectation
on the rim of the great Pacific Ocean.
Out past the breaking surf
in deeps my line cannot reach
no doubt swims a fish or two
but here the sea curls and froths
retreats – returns
churns the sand
surely no fish would choose to swim
in this washing machine.

But, just maybe
into this watery waste
some foolish bream will stray
so I'll persist
for it is a pleasant way
to spend a thriftless day.
I swing back the rod, impel the bait
into the breaking sea. It drops
too close I'm sure
so hope is shallow.
I make taught the line, gaze out across the bay
where the horizon ties the headlands
dark against a pinking sky
and feel, through a tenuous thread
the pulsing brine.

Far, far out swarms a plankton soup
scooped into minuscule mouths
that feed silvery shoals
suddenly scattered
by snapping jaws
in turn, in turn
up to the sinuous shark.
And, what scaly snow
falls to dark depths
forms food for clawed and crabby things.
Thus the void is filled
while above the breathing swell
gulls and terns flutter in anticipation
and I am tied to this mystery
by a fishing line.

Tiger Snake

It lay, across the path
that lead away from the riffles
where the small trout played
to the deep mysterious lairs
of the slab-sided lunkers of my dreams.

A shiny bar of bronze
banded with gold
each scale glistened
smoothly strong
as long as my rod
as thick as my wrist
the head raised
in contemptuous arrogance
black bead eyes searched me
a flickering tongue
tasted my air – unimpressed.

For a time unmeasured
we two were tied
it, in indifferent possession
of its space
I, in thrall
(beauty had a stronger grip
than fear)

Sydney Funnel-web

who would suspect that an assassin
lurked in a shoe under my bed
but I felt its prickle
and tipped it out

defiant, it raised up
full two inches of brave black knight
pranced a flamenco
holding up high two shining scimitars
as might a banderillero
ready to strike a mighty bull to loud *olés*
but this tiny chevalier
undaunted, faced a foe
whose big toe was as tall
and weighed ten thousand times more
– but his no empty threat
for the dew that hung
upon his swords
could kill one twice my size

had he not earned respect
enough to spare his life?
should I have waved him on his errand way?
but fear overrules nobility
I struck him with my shoe
scooped the hairy corpse
into a matchbox
and rushed with a prayer to
the hospital where I lay
limb enswathed hour on hour
till reassured – I would live
to tell of my encounter
with *Atrax robustus*

Violet

elusive colour
painters get you wrong
you are not that hybrid purple
offspring of red and blue
but pure, nothing but yourself
beyond blue, further than indigo
ecstatic deepness
on the edge of perception
rare, nature does not splash you in
swathes across sky; sea and plain
but keeps you precious, small
so we crave more
more of the emperor's robe
more of the amethystine jewel
more of the shy, nodding flower
quietly cloaking woodland banks
that presages spring
and
the brief blush that comes
when the sun is done
and garish pink fades to its bed
the finale before the black curtain falls.

In Praise of Grey

Some say grey is tiresome, useless
a stain across the spectrum.
No artist would concur.
Grey is not a lack of colour
rather, a harmony of subtle hues
to those with eyes that penetrate
beyond the obvious
that would dwell in wonder
on the wild dove's breast
or see, in the bark of a tree
patterns drawn in tones
without number.
Recently, I looked anew
on a London winter sky
through skeletal trees
a milky lacework
more delicate than any
nimble fingers could knot.
Would a firmament of
uniform blue
have held my gaze?
Grey does not stand in neutrality
between white and black
those extremes of nothingness
but glides about the pallet
among soft shades of pinks
blues, yellows.

A humble beauty
that delights in flattering
primary colours
but rewards
those who borrow time
to contemplate
its quiet voice.

5

Exile: Spiritual

Truth is a Doe in the Woods

seldom seen by those
who seek her
with heavy tread.

Some brag, *We have her*
return from the hunt
with trumpet calls –
display a carcass.

Fools! Truth is a living thing
The proud cannot own her –
she slips silent away.

To know her –
go alone in the first light.
Unexpected, she will come.

The Divine Hunter

A pantoum inspired by Francis Thompson's *The Hound of Heaven*

He never relented the chase
like a wolf on the scent of its prey
the outrage of His grace
hunted me night and day

like a wolf on the scent of its prey
though I ran through paths of thorn
He hunted me night and day
impervious to my scorn

though I ran through paths of thorn
He would not surrender my soul
impervious to my scorn
He trawled me out of Sheol

He would not surrender my soul
by the outrage of His grace
He trawled me out of Sheol
He never relented the chase

The Worm that Lives in the Eye

On hearing David Attenborough interviewed

there is a worm which lives in the human eye
and they go blind in Africa
where then a loving God?

with rows of tiny teeth
exquisite   designed
to mine flesh

bringer of night
who made thee
if not He
whose word brought light
whose whim
painted the butterfly wing
composed melody
in a dull brown bird
made the rhinoceros absurd
gave
food with flavour
gardens of fragrance
formed
creatures from clay
with words to praise
yet
also the worm

Job's question 'why?'
still lies unanswered
the potter gave no wherefore
to the pot
in His redeeming art
all things are integral
      even the worm
but if the greed of genes
formed us
unredeemed
then a worm in the eye
has as much place in things
as the most saintly being
what could it matter then
if a man loses his sight?
there is nothing to see
but night

Accident or Design?

who is the designer and who the designed?
was it some capricious accident
that worked to mould the DNA
from an amorphous slime
and gave genesis to all life?
and is mankind the manifestation
of a chance that necessitated
our genes to survive by
giving rise to thought
and all of art, science, good and ill
have no meaning and no will
except to perpetuate a chemical chain?
then when and what selective gain
made this adapted brain
invent for itself
an inventor?

or was it all intended
by a mind infinite in scope
eternally there
before the bang that time began
every detail planned and each twist
of fate foretold
in a word
encoded in a helix
that unfolds to form
a being that speaks
with a purpose to fulfil
and a will
to praise its maker

The Love Gene

Can there be a selfish gene
for selfless love?
Its only function
procreation?
Then love does not love at all
but is red in tooth and claw
a happenstance that gave
to some ancient Eve and Adam
the means to supplant
brute Neanderthals.
Its kindly countenance
camouflaged arrogance.

Or was the universe
brought to being:
by Love
for Love
that Love
should be complete
and the meek
claim inheritance.

Forgiveness

that gift which enriches the giver
yet is so hard to give
indivisible
to forgive in part
is not to forgive at all
but can I forgive in heart alone?
or must it be known
to the forgiven?
and how could I be sure
of its acceptance?
and what the cost to me
to yield up
long-nurtured bitterness
what hollow would it leave?

if forgiveness were simple:
costless words voiced in mumbled pride
no enmity could remain
and no lawyer would grow rich
but hate feeds on pride
sweet deceit of injuries
real or perceived
erodes the soul

Good Friday

the new 'enlightenment' has decreed
neo-Darwinism the official creed
though some other religions may exist
provided they are from the ancient east
or paganism, or New Age at least
(with Islam – best not to interfere
the consequences could be drear)
indeed, such beliefs the law protects
from criticism by Christian sects
but against Jesus, feel entirely free
to publish any blasphemy
no court in this land will let them sue
among judiciary believers are few
and so, in many imaginative ways
through art, poetry and in plays
Christ is spat on in mockery
just as he was on Calvary

Improbability

Lord
in the face of all that is probable
that is scientifically predictable
you did that which should be impossible
when you raised to life
He from whom life had been
stripped with scourge and thorn and nail.
That a grave-bound corpse
should again walk, talk and teach
is miracle enough
and yet that was not all.

That the one who submitted
himself to death's ordeal
was none other than the Word
through whom
disciples and tormentors alike
and the entire universe
came into being
is a wonder of cosmological
dimensions
but that is not all.

That he should endure this for me
who is at one in sin
with they that caused his agony
is a thing beyond all philosophising.
Oh Lord perform one more wonder:
Make even my stubborn heart
obediently understand
Your Love.

Unspoken

the words that pierce most deep are those unsaid
when cold indifference, love's debt denies
it is for those most dear, most tears are shed

angry words are cudgels about the head
and the heart is stabbed by cruel chastise
but words that pierce most deep are those unsaid

by they whose fondness ledger is writ in red
for indifference surely spells 'despise'
and for those beloved, most tears are shed

we hoard endearments till a loved one's dead
then before deaf mourners eulogise
when the words that caused the grief were those unsaid

laughter with total strangers may be shared
they see the mask not that which underlies
only with those most loved, may tears be shed

it was through my ingratitude He bled
for my peace, my solace, to dry my eyes
yet words that pierced His side were words unsaid
and for me He loved, His blood was shed.

Poor Man Hiro

The Japanese have a word for it
Hikikomori
A recluse in his own home
driven by shame, an acquired shyness, so intense
he hid from the world. For the nine years we lived next door
I saw him perhaps five times. Was warned that he would not want to talk.
Still, we left notes inviting friendship.
But over the years he retreated further, his house derelict
his garden a wilderness where he was sometimes glimpsed.

Once as a boy in a London suburb, we found, lying among long grass
by the allotments, a small deer, a ruby stream out of its nostrils
the soft hair warm to the stroke. Hit by a car we surmised
but surprised that this timid creature had remained behind
when the estate spread across the pastures.
It explained the cloven prints in the mud – not the devil after all
and the eaten cabbages and beans
but to know too late that such a being had lived among us
had we but seen it furtive in the dawn…

We watched for Hiro, noted his mail removed from the box
his light come on in the evening, but never any rubbish put out!
Would that have been too clear a sign for those who hunted him?
Neighbours exchanged notes of sightings
so we knew he survived
until the morning when the locksmiths came from the bank
with a sheriff and police. Later they ribboned off his house.
We enquired anxiously, for the sake of conscience
of the pale young policeman: he had still been warm when found.

Grey Mutton

They float in on the tide, strand on the shore
in their dozens; hundreds; thousands.
Horrid reminders of mortality.
Once skimmed weightless,
sliding down smooth swells
effortless
from the Tasman to the Bering and back
alive to every gust and sway of breeze
mystic spirits of the sea.
Now sodden grey lumps of putridity
that dogs sniff and leave
and we grieve
for what? The waste?
But nature is generous in death
as it is abundant in birth.
The dead nurture the living
the past feeds the future.
This sand-strewn mortuary
speaks of our own ephemerality
death is in our DNA.

We make cruel tragedy
of a fallen sparrow
deny death any place here.
Perhaps far away
over the ocean's deeps
      or in a nursing home.

Why should we reject
that which merely takes back
what we are lent?
Night is a portal
to a different day
at whose dawn we shall rise
float on wings in eternal skies
swallowed up in victory
where then the sting?

Philosopher's Stone

Nietzsche pronounced God dead
Russell danced on His grave
Sartre declared
we are free to believe
anything
except in Him

I went to the tomb
saw the void filled
with abstrusions
amazing minds had wrought
that they might copulate
with whomever they please.

Dawkins preaches
'Righteous is the man
who passes on his genes'
and the only sins
are to worship the deity
and commit that of which
Singer disapproves.

Yet logic-forged nails
fail to pin Him
who made the rules
by which games of mind are played.

Antithetic to all reason
He lives;
therefore I am.

Resurrection Sunday

the mudeye* lives content
in the only home it has known
fog-visioned in a one-layered world
among the detritus of years
all it knows or cares to know
is in this mire
tales of a world above
dreams of fools

the light calls
light the darkness never knew
that gives life to all things above
and beneath the sediment

its time come
this instar climbs
a bending reed to sighs
of wind-shaken leaves
rests, exposed
to unbearable brightness
awaits the promise

it is finished!

the curtain rends
emergent
arching from the husk-tomb
of larval life
bright shining as the sun
crystal lattice wings
stretch like pinioned arms

it rises

* mudeye – the dragonfly larva

6

Exile: Whimsical

How the Frogmouth Got Its Name

Mopoke looked down from her perch up high
Saw a fat green frog come hopping by.
'Stay a while my portly friend,' she said.
'Let's talk together – perhaps break bread.'

'Your invite is uncommonly kind
It grieves me that it must be declined
The frog choir meets at the lake today
I sing bass – so I must not delay.'

'Surely you can stop just a short while
This lonely life I find such a trial
Let me just come down for little talk
While you take rest from your weary walk.'

'I hope I do not seem to be rude
But do not mopokes see frogs as food?
If I should I let you get too near
You might be tempted to eat me, I fear.'

'Oh, that is a hurtful thing to say.
Tell me, how could I manage that I pray?
For you are so big and round and sleek
No way could you fit in my small beak.'

'Now were it strong and hooked and grand
Just like an eagle's, I could understand
Your worry. Or a pelican's great bill
That a hundred fat frogs would not fill.

And if I possessed the heron's spear
You might be wise to run from here –
But tell me, does mine look so cruel?
Is it not a poor pathetic tool?'

Now frogs are brought up to be polite
Though, between you and me, they're far from bright
While mopokes though dull grey of feather
Are in fact, fiendishly clever.

So frog, not wishing to seem boorish
Said, 'Very well.' – I told you he was foolish.
Then the mopoke beside the frog alighted
'To meet with you sir, I am most delighted.'

'Excuse me, I've been awake since dawn,'
Said mopoke as she began to yawn.
Her mouth that had seemed till then quite small
Began to open – so wide – so tall.

The frog observed with some foreboding
It was big enough to fit a toad in.
And still it continued to open more
Like an automatic garage door –

No other bird's beak can open that wide –
The frog – it easily fitted inside.
So that's how the frogmouth got its name
For 'mopoke' and 'frogmouth' are the same.

Moral:

Now little froglets listen and learn
Invitations from strangers always spurn.
Remember poor frog in the mopoke's tummy
And hop off home to tell your mummy.

Aliens

among themselves
they communicate constantly
in unfathomable hieroglyphs
on tablets
to me – if at all –
as to a child or imbecile
of things I cannot comprehend
of a world – their world
beyond my imagining
where machines
supply needs
for joy and play
perhaps love as well
nourished on dreams
and food from factories
their skin, casually displayed
is coloured indelibly
and delicate parts
pierced with
darts that would
cause me pain
there can be no bridging
the gap with music, play or art
we have no words in common
and they will not learn ours
today, they are strange intruders
tomorrow this land will be theirs.

Boat People: 1800

The way they behave in our land, shows
they have no wish to integrate.
They insist their women
cover those bits of their anatomy
that ours feel free to expose and show
our girls no respect.
Some of their men are guilty of rape
and our youths have been attacked
in the places we used to feel safe
even on the beach. They say it's only
a small minority of them
but its up to their community
to take responsibility for their extremists.
They live as though they had never left
their homeland: eat strange food
would, if they could change our beautiful
land to be like the one they left behind.
They only live among their own kind
make no attempt to learn our tongue.
If they get their way, would force on us
their strange beliefs
and foreign laws.
Yet still they complain
that it is we who are hostile.
If they don't like the way we live
why don't they return from where they came?
Did our country not take them in
when they, in desperation
fled poverty and persecution?
It simply won't work, try as we might
for we are black
and they are white.

Real Estate

It's no McMansion, rather bijou
but home to me

It's no McMansion, rather cosy
windows rattle, doors won't shut
showing wear but home to me

It's no McMansion, rather modest
windows rattle, doors won't shut
paint is peeling, the plumbing's kaput
getting old, yet home to me

It's no McMansion, rather compact
windows rattle, doors won't shut
paint is peeling, the plumbing's kaput
the roof leaks, the guttering's rusted
still, it's home to me

It's no McMansion, rather pokey
windows rattle, doors won't shut
paint is peeling, the plumbing's kaput
the roof leaks, guttering's rusted,
it's got termites and the boilers busted
I'll sell the bugger!

The Perfect Pet

Could you, would you, love a slug?
Enjoy a slippery, slimy hug?

I have no itchy hair or fur
never bark, snarl or even purr

but silent mucus bubbles blow.
I'd fetch a stick if you should throw

and drop it gently at your shoe
though it may take a month or two.

Oh, such a faithful friend I'd make
just feed me lettuce and stale cake.

I will never scratch nor spit nor bite
but snuggle up to you at night.

I'd leave no smelly doo and that
but lay silver trails across your mat.

Though some may think me cold and wet
I would make a marvellous pet.

Together we'd keep the planet clean.
Did you know my blood is green?

So won't you grant my dearest wish
and give this slug a hug and kiss?

The Answer To All Your Storage Problems

It said in letters convincingly bold
and to this concept I was entirely sold.
We would soon have a place to store
all our clutter and even more:
clothes; shoes; winter doonas; spare sheets
books; records; toys and baby seats.
Oh what bliss upon that day
when each possession is stacked away.
To open the crate, it said on the label,
first, place it flat upon a table
use the special key, no other kind,
which wrapped in plastic, inside you'll find.
With patience's limit all but reached
by means of an axe the seal was breached
and onto the floor an avalanche spilled
till with wood and metal the room was filled
and deep in the pile I finally found
a book of instructions – paperbound.
There was written every language and script
Mandarin, Arabic, Hebrew, Cyrillic
Klingon even, and ancient Rhenish
finally one that was almost English:
1 Please to hold the backpiece in one hand
      be sure the toggle-hole reaches the band.
2 Then with the other hand tightly hold
      the right flexirunner – do not fold.
3 Now with another hand please take
      and scinter the left side shelving brake.

4 Next without slackening any grip
        (on no account let the firdle slip)
        firmly fix with the bolt, nine-sided
        using a spong-head spanner (not provided).

And so on and on for pages and pages
I persevered through frequent rages.
My family begged me to desist.
'Just one more piece,' I would insist
as I kicked the cat and beat my son,
'they said by a child this could be done
and finish I will should it cost me my life.'
The front door slammed as she left: my wife.
Through long nights and through the days
I hammered, screwed and glued a thousand ways
until the final instruction was attained
and only twenty-four pieces on the floor remained
but before me was not the elegant creation
pictured in colour on the front of the carton
but a monstrous thing, hideously confusing
that emanated feelings hostile, accusing.
So I hurried and fetched from cupboard and closet
all I could find and on the 'thing' did deposit
clothes; shoes; winter doonas; spare sheets
books; records; toys and baby seats.
I made an enormous funeral pyre
then laughed and danced as the flames rose higher
for I realised that, when all was done
my storage problems indeed were gone.

Lifecycle

lying
crying
feeding
needing
walking
talking
following
hollering
learning
earning
driving
thriving
caring
pairing
seeding
breeding
deceiving
leaving
succeeding
receding
ageing
raging
ailing
failing
needing
feeding
lying
crying

Immigrants

We are not welcome here
you make that clear
are not even subtle in your disdain
say outright you want us out
persecute us
why? What have we ever done wrong?
Oh, we know all the excuses
the fabricated charges:
'we displace locals from their homes.'
Where is the evidence?
We smell and get together in noisy gangs.
I have news for you
you suffer from BO.
And so what that we are sociable
have cheerful gatherings of our clan?
You don't see us in the pubs getting drunk.
Have you forgotten: we were brought here
to help farmers?
Even now we eke out a living
where 'Aussies' will not go.
You claim we're a threat:
to whom? Have we ever been caught
with blood on our hands?
But we know the real reason:
is because we are different
we are brown and foreign
though have been here
as long as most of you
were born here in fact

so this is our home too
and we are not going anywhere
so just get used to us:
learn to love Indian mynahs.

Clichés: Avoid Them Like the Plague

Proust, that much revered French muse,
said, 'A cliché never ever use.'
They were the bane of his existence,
but still crop up with great persistence.

Have you ever stopped to wonder why
the breeze in the trees gives always a sigh
the sun always shines on golden corn
blackbirds sing to welcome the dawn?

Why with ardour passion always burns;
and eventually the worm, it turns?
But it really saves a lot of thought
to employ a phrase well known and short.

Should it not be be horses for courses?
Who can withstand such irresistible forces
of expressions that fit so well in context,
and spring to mind in an autonomous reflex?

Like a favourite hat or well-worn shoes
clichés are so comfortable to use.
But Proust would say there's just one perfect word
so to repeat the same ones is quite absurd.

He wrote only in phrases complex and new,
but then those who read him are so very few.

To a Girl Seen in the Park

with apologies to Cornford

Why walk through trees with plugs in your ear
        Missing so much and so much?
Sweet teenager who looks so dear
        Must you constantly listen to sounds so drear
When the breeze whispers love songs for those who would hear
        And the thrush serenades its sky-blue clutch
Why walk through trees with a stopped-up ear
        Missing so much and so much?

Genesis by Committee

In the beginning the heavenly committee met
to consider an agenda the Chairman had set
for the Earth was without any form
void and darkness was upon the deep.
'Let there be light,' the Chairman loudly proposed
'that surely is something that will not be opposed.'
'Before I can agree to second your motion,'
said an Angel, 'though please don't doubt my devotion
but in order to give it our full consideration
we need from you more information.'
Another concurred, 'Yes, where do we get this light
and what will it cost? You know our budget is tight.'
Just then Satan came bustling in through the door
balancing papers and coffee which he spilt on the floor.
'Sorry I'm late again,' said he breathlessly
'but I had some important business, you see.'
The Chairman peered over his glasses: 'Indeed!'
'Yes, so if you could just bring me up to speed.'
The secretary read out the minutes thus far
while Satan squeezed himself in next to the Chair
'Oh, I am not sure this "light" will hit the mark
frankly, all my best work is done in the dark.'
Chairman thundered, 'Earth is not intended for you.'
'But we should accommodate the minority view,'
opined another Angel to widespread nods
'else we might be seen to be acting like gods.'
And so they discussed whether light might be good
and what style, what colour; how bright; whether it should
be made to shine from the sky or out of the sea.

They still had not finished when they broke for tea
after which Gabriel in a conciliatory vein
proposed they adjourn and meet sometime again
while a subcommittee of angels, expenses paid
would investigate how this 'light' should be made
until consensus was reached nothing should be done
this went to a vote which was comprehensively won.
In vain did the Chairman his omniscience aver
though one Angel did agree if it were left up to her
he could create light – but the majority held sway.
'Twas the evening and morning of the first day.

Zed (or Zee?)

I read somewhere
that children with names
late in the alphabet
grow feeling neglected –
by always being last
so little wonder the zebra
though more striking –
beautiful even
should be the timid
retiring relation of the horse
but then
does it apply to the zebu? or zho?
even the zander?
and why was Zeta Zecharia
with her dark cascading curls
and haughty eyes
the most popular girl in form three?

www.ingramcontent.com/pod-product-compliance
Lightning Source LLC
Chambersburg PA
CBHW070919080526
44589CB00013B/1358